Guidelines for Medication Administration: An Instructional Program for Training Unlicensed Personnel to Give Medications in Out-of-Home Child Care, Schools and Camp Settings: Student Handbook, Ed. 5

Colorado Division of Child Care, Colorado Department of Public Health and Environment, et al.

The BiblioGov Project is an effort to expand awareness of the public documents and records of the U.S. Government via print publications. In broadening the public understanding of government and its work, an enlightened democracy can grow and prosper. Ranging from historic Congressional Bills to the most recent Budget of the United States Government, the BiblioGov Project spans a wealth of government information. These works are now made available through an environmentally friendly, print-on-demand basis, using only what is necessary to meet the required demands of an interested public. We invite you to learn of the records of the U.S. Government, heightening the knowledge and debate that can lead from such publications.

Included are the following Collections:

Budget of The United States Government
Presidential Documents
United States Code
Education Reports from ERIC
GAO Reports
History of Bills
House Rules and Manual
Public and Private Laws

Code of Federal Regulations
Congressional Documents
Economic Indicators
Federal Register
Government Manuals
House Journal
Privacy act Issuances
Statutes at Large

Guidelines for
Medication Administration:
An Instructional Program for
Training Unlicensed Personnel to
Give Medications in
Out-of-Home Child Care,
Schools and Camp Settings

STUDENT HANDBOOK

2008
Fifth Edition

cdhs
Colorado Department of Human Services
people who help people

Colorado Department
of Public Health
and Environment

MCHB
Maternal and Child Health Bureau

U.S. DEPARTMENT OF HEALTH & HUMAN SERVICE
HRSA
Health Resources & Services Administration

Funding resource provided by the Department of Human Services, Division of Child Care and the
Health Systems Development in Child Care Grant Healthy Child Care Colorado Initiative (#5 H24 MC 00021-05)

Guidelines for Medication Administration:
An Instructional Program for
Training Unlicensed Personnel to
Give Medications in
Out-of-Home Child Care, Schools and Camp Settings

2008
Fifth Edition

RECOGNIZED AND APPROVED BY:

Colorado Department of Education

201 East Colfax Avenue
Denver, Colorado 80203

Colorado Department of Public Health and Environment
Healthy Child Care Colorado
4300 Cherry Creek Drive South.
Denver, Colorado 80246

Colorado State Board of Nursing
1560 Broadway, Suite 670
Denver, Colorado 80202

Department of Human Services,
Division of Child Care
1575 Sherman St.
Denver, Colorado 80203

The Children's Hospital
School Health Program
13123 E. 16th Avenue
Aurora, Colorado 80045

This manual may be downloaded by approved medication administration trainers at:

Qualistar Early Learning
www.qualistar.org

Medication Administration Instructional Program
STUDENT HANDBOOK
TABLE OF CONTENTS

STUDENT HANDBOOK
TABLE OF CONTENTS

GUIDELINES FOR MEDICATION ADMINISTRATION IN OUT-OF-HOME CHILDCARE, SCHOOLS AND CAMP PROGRAMS

Purpose: The purpose of this Medication Administration Instructional Program is to teach school, child care and camp staff basic information about administering medication to infants, toddlers, preschool and school-aged children.

Goal: The goal of this training is to ensure safe and accurate administration of oral, topical, inhaled and emergency medications to infants and children.

Student Participant Responsibilities
At the end of the training the student participant will:
♦ Recognize the responsibility in giving medications safely and accurately.
♦ Understand the general purpose of medication.
♦ Demonstrate proper hand washing and standard (universal) precautions.
♦ Demonstrate competency in storing, measuring the correct dosage and administering different types of medications using various medication measuring devices, e.g., oral, inhaled, nebulized, eye, ear, nose, topical, and emergency medications.
♦ Demonstrate accurate record keeping, including proper documentation of all doses of medication administration.
♦ Describe medication incidents and how they can be avoided.
♦ If applicable, describe the student's role in performing the delegated task of medication administration, under the supervision of the RN.
♦ Use resources appropriately.
♦ Pass a written test
♦ Receive a certificate of completion

Instructional Program Requirements:

Instructor:
A licensed registered nurse (RN) or physician familiar with
♦ Colorado laws and regulations regarding the storage and administration of medication.
♦ Colorado Division of Child Care licensing information, if applicable.
♦ Administering medications to infants, toddlers and school aged children.

Time:
Minimum of 4 hours

Student to Instructor Ratio
♦ Recommended 10 participants per instructor
♦ Maximum of 12-15 participants per instructor

Medications *Covered* in this Instructional Program

This course includes the following types of medications:

Typical and Routine Medications for Short Term Use
- Antibiotics
- Eye or ear drops
- Non-narcotic pain medications
- Ointments and creams used as a *treatment* for a skin condition.
- Over-the-counter medications

Medications Taken on A Regular Basis for Chronic Health Conditions
- Asthma medications, including inhalers and nebulizers
- ADD/ADHD medications
- Antidepressants
- Oral seizure medications
- Routine heart medications
- Medications for muscle spasms

Emergency Medications
- Antihistamines
- Epi-Pen®

*Individualized health care plan (health care provider written instructions)
are necessary for children with nebulizer treatments
and emergency medications.*

Medications *Not Covered* by this Instructional Program

The following medications are <u>NOT</u> covered by this course:

- Medication that requires nursing or medical judgment
- As needed medications for health conditions e.g., asthma, diabetes
- Injectables other than Epi-Pen®, e.g., glucagon or insulin
- Medication that requires taking blood pressure or pulse before or after giving medication.
- Medications given by special feeding tubes.
- Rectal medications.
- Experimental medications
- Homeopathic and herbal preparations

*These medications are to be administered by an RN
or the child's parent/guardian.*

There are occasions when the RN consultant or school nurse in a one-to-one situation may delegate these medications for the child with a stable health condition. This is determined on an individual basis, and only with a current, detailed health care plan.

The added responsibility of providing medications in schools, child care or camp programs creates a potential health risk for the child and liability for the caregiver. Ideally parent or guardians should make every attempt to administer medications to their children.

RIGHTS AND RESPONSIBILITIES

Delegation and the Colorado Nurse Practice Act

The Colorado Nurse Practice Act is the law that licenses and regulates the practice of nursing and states what a registered nurse (RN) and a licensed practical nurse (LPN) may do in their practice. This law says that people who are not nurses cannot perform tasks that require a nursing license. In order to meet the growing health need in the community, a *delegatory clause* was added to the Colorado Nurse Practice Act in 1992 that permits an RN to delegate the responsibility of medication administration and special health procedures to other people under certain conditions.

In Colorado, medications are legally administered by an RN <u>or</u> by an unlicensed person, e.g., school, child care or camp personnel, to whom the RN has delegated the task of giving medication. A Licensed Practical Nurse (LPN) may administer medications under the supervision of a physician or a registered nurse. However, a Licensed Practical Nurse (LPN) **may not** delegate medication administration to unlicensed personnel.

This training is designed to give school, child care and camp personnel basic information on the steps involved in the administration of medication to children.

Training alone does not mean delegation. **After completing this medication administration training, school/child care personnel must again demonstrate competency in their ability to administer medication <u>to the RN delegating the task of medication administration</u>.** The delegating RN must review and document staff competencies in medication administration, at least annually.

Delegation means that a registered nurse (RN) may assign to a child care provider or school staff member the task of medication administration and/or the ability to perform special health procedures. The RN is responsible for the care that is provided.

However, school/child care personnel may not be delegated tasks that require nursing judgement or be delegated nursing care needs that require an assessment by a registered nurse.

Special note:
♦ School or child care staff <u>may not</u> further delegate medication administration or another special health procedure to another individual.
♦ The task may not be changed without permission of the delegating RN.
♦ At any time, the RN consultant may withdraw delegation if, in the opinion of delegating RN, the person is unable or fails to perform the task as directed by the RN.
♦ The RN may withdraw the delegation of a particular medication/special health procedure, if there is a change in the stability of the child's health condition or there is a change in the nature of the medication.

Exception to Delegation: The licensed family child care provider is exempt

Reference: Chapter XIII of the Rules and Regulations Regarding the Delegation of Nursing Function, Colorado Nurse Practice Act.

The decision to delegate can only be made by the RN in a given situation. It cannot be made by a parent, physician or program administrator.

<u>Student notes</u>

from the delegation requirement when administering routine medications to children in their family child care homes. To be exempt they must:

- Have successfully completed a medication administration instructional program that is approved by the Colorado Department of Human Services;
- Have daily physical contact with the parent or guardian of the Client to whom medications are administered;
- Administer only routine medications and only in compliance with rules promulgated by the state Board of Human Services;
- In emergency situations requiring the administration of unit dose epinephrine, comply with any protocols written by the prescribing health care professional; and
- Administer a nebulized inhaled medication only in compliance with protocols written by the prescribing health care professional that identify the need for such administration.

Reference:
Board of Nursing 3 CCR 716-1; CHAPTER XIII; RULES AND REGULATIONS REGARDING THE DELEGATION OF NURSING TASKS

Other Important Laws

American with Disabilities Act (ADA)

The ADA requires that programs make reasonable accommodations for children with mental or physical disabilities and chronic illness. Children in schools, child care, camp programs and other community settings, can no longer be excluded on the basis of a disability. The program must consider each case individually and comply with the requirements of ADA.

Confidentiality

Each program should have a confidentiality policy. Information about a child's health condition must not be discussed with anyone unless the parents have given their written permission. Medication should be administered as privately as possible and the type of medication should never be mentioned or discussed with anyone else.

A breach of confidentiality, the sharing of information without written permission, can result in serious consequences.
Such disclosure can cause the child and family great distress and are possible grounds for lawsuit.

The Purposes of Medication are to:
- Prevent illness
- Relieve symptoms
- **Control or cure health problems**

How Medications Work in the Body

Compared to adults, children, especially from birth to 3 years of age, are immature and process medicines ineffectively. Children are more susceptible to medication side effects, overdoses and allergies. Children are smaller than adults, and need less medicine to obtain the desired effect.

Medications can produce both desired and undesired results.

Three Types of Undesired Results

- **Side effects** are natural, expected and predictable reactions of the drug. Most side effects are minor and are not cause for great concern.

- **Adverse reactions** are unexpected and potentially harmful. If an adverse reaction is observed in a child, the parent should be notified immediately.

- **Allergic reactions** are difficult to predict. Allergic reactions may involve different types of symptoms, e.g., mild redness of the skin, itching and rashes or swelling. If an allergic reaction is observed in a child, call the parent immediately and request contact with the health care provider.

A severe form of an allergic reaction is anaphylaxis

THIS IS A LIFE THREATENING CONDITION

CALL 911

Prescription medications require a written authorization by a person with prescriptive authority.

According to the Colorado Board of Pharmacy, persons with prescriptive authority include:

- Physicians, MD or DO (Doctor of Osteopathy)
- Podiatrists, DPM
- Dentists, DDS or DMD
- Advance Practice Nurse; Nurse Practitioner or Clinical Nurse Specialist
- Physician Assistant who has direction of a physician or written protocol

Controlled substances are prescription medications that are under the jurisdiction of the Federal Drug Enforcement Agency. These medications present a greater than usual risk of becoming habit forming or of being sold and used illegally. They also have special counting and storage requirements.

Over-the-Counter (OTC) medications may be purchased without a prescription. Like prescription medications, OTC's can be very dangerous to a child, if given incorrectly.

OTC Cough and Cold Preparations In January 2008, the American Academy of Pediatrics (AAP) supported a public health advisory put out by the US Food And Drug Administration. This advisory recommended that OTC cough and cold medications should not be used for infants and children under age 2 because of the risk of life threatening side effects.

It is recommended that parents discuss the use of OTC medications with their health care provider before giving any medications to their child. Parents should be especially careful in giving OTC medications to an infant. Giving a child more than one cold or cough medicine to treat different symptoms can be dangerous. Some of the same ingredients may be in each product. Also, many of these medicines contain acetaminophen. Read labels carefully.

Over-the counter medications administered in the school or child care program require written authorization from the health care provider with prescriptive authority and parent written permission.

Blanket Permission Forms are not acceptable for most OTC medications.

Over-the-counter ointments and creams such as sunscreen, lip balm, skin creams and diaper ointments that are used for *preventive* purposes **do not** require a written authorization from the health care provider with prescriptive authority. However, parent written permission is necessary. If the skin is broken or an allergic reaction is observed, discontinue use and notify the parent.

Over-the-counter ointments and creams used as a treatment for a skin condition such as broken skin, severe diaper rash or eczema requires a written authorization from the health care provider and written parent permission.

Homeopathic medicines are drug products made by homeopathic pharmacies. These remedies are made from many sources, including plants, minerals or animals. They are most often sold over-the-counter.

Herbal preparations have one or more active ingredients in them that are taken from plants. They are simply drugs in a dilute form. They are sold over-the-counter.

No dosage guidelines exist for the administration of herbal or botanical preparations to young and school-aged children.

Homeopathic medication and herbal preparations are not included in this Medication Administration Training. Therefore, school and child care personnel may not administer these without special delegation by the supervising RN

Medications come in different forms and dosages. Instructions must be read and followed very carefully.

<u>Oral</u> medications are given by mouth.

♦ **Tablets**
 - <u>Chewable tablets</u> must be chewed and then swallowed.
 - <u>Uncoated and coated tablets</u> are swallowed whole and are not chewed.
 - <u>Scored tablets</u> may be halved or split in two to give the appropriate dosage. The tablet should be split in two by the pharmacist or parent
 - <u>Quick dissolve strips</u> dissolve instantly when placed in a child's mouth <u>Quick Dissolving tablets</u> also dissolve quickly when placed in the mouth

♦ **Capsules** are taken by mouth and swallowed whole. Do not crush, chew or take apart.

♦ **Sprinkles are contained in capsules. The contents of the capsule are taken apart and sprinkled on food, as directed on the instructions**

♦ **Liquids**
 - <u>Suspensions</u> are fluid substances with solid particles. They separate when left standing and must be shaken well before administration. These medications usually need refrigeration.
 - <u>Syrup or Elixir</u> is a sweetened liquid that contains dissolved medication. Refrigerating oral liquid medications may make them taste better.

<u>Inhalants</u> **are medications that release a medicated mist or powder. These include:**
♦ **Nasal spray** delivers medication into the nose through a spray.
♦ **Metered dose inhalant** is inhaled through the mouth with the use of various adapters or mouthpieces.
♦ **Respiratory nebulizer machine** delivers liquid medication in a fine mist.

<u>Topical</u> medications include eye drops, eye ointments, ear drops, and ointments, creams and patches that are applied to the skin.

<u>Injectable</u> medications are administered by an RN <u>or</u> individually delegated to school or child care staff member(s) by the RN consultant or school nurse.

Note: Asthma management and the administration of inhaled medications including nebulizer treatments will be covered in a separate module of this training curriculum.

Severe allergy management will be covered in a separate module of this training curriculum

General Guidelines
- Prescription medication must **ALWAYS** be kept in the original labeled bottle or container.
- Over-the-counter medication must also be stored in the original container and clearly labeled with the child's name.
- Store medications and supplies in a clean, secure and locked area.
- Keep medications in a cool, dry, dark place.
- Return to the parent any medication containers with labels that cannot be read.
- The parent or guardian is responsible for bringing the medication to the school or program. Children <u>should not</u> transport medication.
- Notify parents when the medication supply is low.

Refer to the "Sample Policy on Medication Administration "

Controlled Medications
- Store controlled medications in a locked storage area.
  Access to these medications <u>must</u> be limited to delegated staff.
- Count and document the drug amount when it is received, when it is returned to the parent or when it is disposed.

Refrigeration
- The refrigerator is kept in an area that is secure and is not accessible to children or unauthorized persons.
- Store medication in a leak-proof container in a designated area of the refrigerator separated from food <u>*OR*</u> in a separate refrigerator used only for medication.
- Check the temperature inside the refrigerator periodically. The ideal temperature is between 36 - 46 °F.

Expired or Discontinued Medications
- Return to the parent or guardian any expired medications or medications that are no longer being used.
- If the medication has not been picked up within one week of the date of the request, then follow the procedures listed below.
- Medications <u>should not</u> be sent home in a child's backpack or stored within reach of children.

Disposal of Medications
All medications in out-of-home settings no longer being used or expired should ideally be returned to the child's parents for disposal. If this cannot be done staff from the school or child care program should properly dispose of the medication.

According to the Colorado Department of Public Health and Environment, it is no longer recommended that even small quantities of medications be flushed down the drain. Some medicines can disrupt or destroy the useful microorganisms in the sewage treatment system and/or may pass through the system intact and potentially contaminate downstream water resources.

Procedures for stabilizing medications include:
- ◆ Securely wrap unusable or unwanted medications in several layers of newspaper and enclose in a plastic bag or trash bag. Put this bundle in your regular trash.
- ◆ Store trash containing disposed medications out of reach of children and pets until it can be picked up by the trash disposal service and/or taken to the land fill.

Further recommendations from the EPA include information for medication disposal as well:
- ◆ Keep the pharmaceuticals in their original container since the labels may contain safety information, the container is chemically compatible, and the caps are typically water tight and child proof
- ◆ Add a small amount of water to the solid drug or some absorbent material such as kitty litter, sawdust or flour to liquid drugs before recapping. These measures are intended to discourage any unintended use of the drug
- ◆ Double enclose the contained drugs in a bag or any other waste container to prevent immediate identification of a drug container or prevent a glass drug container from breaking during the disposal process.

Refer to the Sample "Disposal Log"

A staff person (or RN) and a witness should document on the "*Medication or Disposal Log*". Include the child's name, date, time, the name of the medicine(s), amount of medicine disposed and the signature of the staff person (or RN) and witness.

Self Carry Medications
In Colorado, children may be allowed to self carry asthma and anaphylaxis medications in school as well as some group care settings. Self administration in these settings refers to situations in which students carry their medication on their person and administer the medication to themselves. There are orders from their healthcare provider, authorization from their parent, and the administration is done in accordance with school district or program policy. Typically this medication is not handled by school or child care personnel nor stored in the program's medication storage area.

Discuss the specifics for these children with your school nurse or nurse consultant.

People in the United States spend millions of dollars on over-the-counter medications, for fever, pain, colds and coughs. Many of these medicines are unnecessary, and in the case of young children, particularly under the age of 5 years, these medications often produce side effects, instead of providing relief to bothersome symptoms.

"The increase in parents working outside the home puts pressure on families, child care providers and health professionals alike to keep children symptom free and in care. As a result, we may tend to reach quickly for over-the-counter remedies to alleviate symptoms; remedies do little, if anything, to help. Not only is much of this medicine not beneficial, but some of it also could be doing harm"
Dr. James M. Poole, MD, FAAP, American Academy of Pediatrics Committee on Early Childhood, Adoption and Dependent Care." Excerpt: Healthy Child Care America, Summer 1999, pg. 4.

Non-prescription Medications for Common Symptoms
♦ If the child is playing and sleeping normally, non-prescription medications are not needed.
♦ Medications should only be given for symptoms that cause significant discomfort, such as repeated coughing or difficulty with sleeping. Parents should consult with the health care provider.
♦ Viral illnesses are best treated with rest, fluids and comfort measures.
♦ Over-the-counter medications are not usually helpful and may be harmful

Antibiotics Use
♦ More than 90% of infections are due to viruses.
♦ Antibiotics have no effect on viruses.
♦ Antibiotics kill bacteria. It is important to complete the full 10-14 days of treatment, even though the child may feel well.
♦ Antibiotics should be given at home whenever possible. This has been made easier now that once and twice daily dosages are available.

Common Antibiotics Used with Children
▪ Amoxicillin
▪ Augmentin®
▪ Erythromycin® mostly used with teens for acne
▪ Keflex® (cephalexin)
▪ Pediazole® (sulfasoxazole and erythromycin)
▪ Zithromax® (azithomycin)

Common Side Effects
▪ Upset stomach, nausea and/or vomiting, diarrhea – any of the above antibiotics can cause side effects, though some are worse than others. Augmentin® and Keflex® seem to be the worst for diarrhea and Erythromycin is the worst for nausea. Vomiting is a much less common side effect of the above medications, though Erythromycin is the worst.
▪ Notify the health care provider for severe or prolonged diarrhea.

Adverse Reaction
Rash or allergic reaction, notify parent and health care provider
Immediately as any of the antibiotics can cause an adverse reaction.

A fever is the body's <u>normal</u> response to an infection. It is important to remember that a fever is only a symptom of an infection, and is not an illness of its own.

The body's average temperature can vary greatly during the day, between 97.6° F. to 99.5° F. Mild elevations between 100° F. to 101° F. can be caused by exercise, excessive clothing, hot bath or hot weather.

An infant less than 4 months of age has a fever
if the temperature is 100° F. (axillary) or greater.

<u>Fever Reducers</u>
♦ For fevers of 100° F. – 102° F. (axillary), cold fluids and removal of outer clothing may be all the child needs to reduce the fever. Sponging is not usually necessary.
♦ Use fever-reducing medicine only if the fever is over 102° F. and if the child is uncomfortable.
♦ Tylenol ® (acetaminophen) may be given every 4-6 hours, but not more often.
♦ Motrin® or Advil® (ibuprofen) may be given every 6-8 hours (longer lasting than Tylenol®).

♦ **DO NOT GIVE ASPIRIN (or products with aspirin) TO CHILDREN.**

♦ **DO NOT GIVE FEVER REDUCERS TO INFANTS LESS THAN 3 MONTHS OF AGE.**

<u>Do not</u> give fever-reducing medications for more than 3 days without further written instructions from the child's health care provider.

<u>Note</u>: Alternating Acetaminophen and Ibuprofen is not recommended.

Remember: you must have written authorization
from the <u>health care provider</u> and <u>parent permission</u>
in order to give these medications.

<u>Return to school or child care:</u> A note from the child's health care provider saying a child may return to school or child care does NOT automatically mean that a child must be accepted back into the program. A program should be using their exclusion guidelines/illness policy, consultation with their school nurse or nurse consultant, as well as the information from the health care provider when determining readmittance for every child.

<u>Exclusion from School or Child Care</u>

Exclude children with fever and behavior changes, unless a health professional says the child may be in school or child care. The child should be well enough to participate in the program and the care of the child should not interfere with the ability to care for the other children in the program.	

Get immediate medical attention for fever when:
- Babies less than 3 months of age with a temperature of 100° F or higher.
- Any child with a temperature of 105° F.or higher.

In the event the parent, emergency contact person or the child's health care provider are not available, the caregiver should contact the nurse consultant or emergency medical services for help.

Myths and Facts about Fever

Reference: Pediatric House Calls Online, B.D. Schmitt, MD, 2nd edition, 2007.

Myth: All fevers are bad for children.

Fact: Fevers turn on the body's immune system. Fevers are one of the body's protective mechanisms. Most fevers are good for children and help the body fight infection.

Myth: Fevers cause brain damage or fevers over 104° F are dangerous.

Fact: Fevers with infections do not cause brain damage. Only body temperature over 108° F. can cause brain damage. The body temperature goes this high only with high environmental temperatures, e.g., if a child is confined in a closed car in hot weather.

Myth: All fevers need to be treated with fever medicine.

Fact: Fevers need to be treated only if they cause discomfort. Usually that means fevers over 102°-103° F.

Myth: Temperatures between 98.7° F. and 100° F. are low-grade fevers.

Fact: The normal temperature changes throughout the day. It peaks in the late afternoon and evening. A low-grade fever is considered to be 100° F. to 102° F.

Myth: The exact number of the temperature is very important.

Fact: How the child looks and how the child is acting is what is important.

Training

Persons involved in medication administration must complete a Medication Administration Instructional Program in order to give medications in schools, child care or camp programs.

Delegation and Supervision

♦ The RN delegating the task of medication administration to school or child care personnel is responsible for the documentation of competency and the ongoing supervision of those persons.

♦ A communication and supervision plan between the delegating RN and the persons involved in the task of medication administration needs to be developed, e.g., on-call, phone or pager availability.

♦ Family child care providers are not required to have delegation from an RN or MD for the administration of routine medications, the medications covered in this training curriculum

1. ## Health Care Provider Written Authorization for Prescription and Non-prescription (over-the counter) Medications:

   - Child's name
   - Name of medication
   - Current date
   - Dosage
   - How to administer (route)
   - Time medication needs to be given while in school or child care
   - Start date and end date
   - Reason for the medicine (may be confidential)
   - Side effects
   - Special instructions or storage information

   Refer to the Sample "Medication Administration Permission" forms

   Note: Blanket permission forms **are not** acceptable.
   The authorization must include the start and end date for the medication as well as the reason the medication is needed.

There is language in the CO American Academy of Pediatrics (AAP) General Health Appraisal form that would allow multiple use of acetaminophen or ibuprofen orders.

Refer to the Sample Forms Section "General Health Appraisal Form"

Refer to the "For Fever Reducer or Pain Reliever" section of the CO AAP General Health Appraisal.

A completed medication authorization form may also be accepted as documentation to administer either acetaminophen or ibuprofen for use multiples times if the following information is provided:
   - Signatures of healthcare provider with prescriptive authority and parent
   - The order states a specific reason when the medication should be given.

- The exact form/concentration of the medication and the dose is listed
- The date of the order and the date to administer the medication are within the time frame of the child's well child visit schedule (e.g. and order written for a 4 month old could be used until the child is 6 months old)
- For school age children medication orders should be renewed at a minimum yearly even though well child visits may be scheduled every two years
- The medication may not be given for more than three consecutive days without additional authorization

Remember: Acetaminophen and ibuprofen are the only medications that may be used multiple times with one authorization for up to three consecutive days ONLY. Other OTC medications can not be administered over time without additional authorizations.

Topical over-the-counter preparations such as sunscreen, diaper creams and ointments <u>do not</u> require written authorization from the health care provider. They may be applied with parent written permission as a preventive measure. If the skin is broken, bleeding or a rash is present, discontinue use, inform the parent or guardian and request written instructions from the health care provider.

2. <u>Parent Written Permission</u>

3. <u>Medication in the Original Pharmacy Labeled Container</u>
   - Child's name
   - Health care provider name
   - Issue date of medicine
   - Name of medication
   - Dosage
   - Route of administration
   - How often to give medicine
   - How many days to give medicine
   - Special instructions
   - Storage requirements
   - Expiration date

   <u>Note:</u> The pharmacy label is *not* the same as the health care provider's written order. Compare the pharmacy label with the written authorization from the health care provider for accuracy <u>before</u> giving medication.

4. <u>Over-the-Counter Medicine Container</u>
   - Child's name
   - Directions for safe use
   - Expiration date
   - List of ingredients

<u>REMEMBER:</u>

		Student Notes

- ✓ Never give medicine without having written instructions <u>and</u> a properly labeled bottle.
- ✓ Never give medicine if all the written information does not match the labeled bottle.
- ✓ Contact the health care provider or RN consultant if you have any questions prior to giving the medicine.

Documentation
The medication log becomes a permanent record and provides legal protection to those administering medication. A medication log page must be filled out for each child <u>and</u> for each medication administered.

Note: Complete a new medication log if there is a change in the child's medication or dosage.

Medication Log Directions
1. The log is a legal document and *must be completed in ink.*
2. If possible, have another trained person, review the completed log for accuracy
3. The **medication log** includes:
   - Child's name
   - Name of medication
   - Date
   - Dosage
   - How the medication is to be given (delivery method or route)
   - Time the medication needs to be given while in school or child care
   - Start date and end date
   - Special instructions or storage information. *For "as needed" medications, be sure you have specific instructions, such as "every 4 hours as needed for repeated coughing, wheezing"*
4. Compare the information on the log with the medication label, <u>before</u> the medication is given.
5. *Document in ink* immediately after the medication is given
   - **Date** and **Time** the medication was given.
   - **Initials** of the person giving the medication. Record only the medication you administered. *If you note something incorrectly on the log, draw a single line through it. Make the correction, initial the right information, sign and date the corrected information. Do not use eraser or use white out.*
6. The **"Comment" section** is used for special situations, e.g., child vomits medication, parent does not bring in medication, or number of pills received.
7. When the health care provider discontinues a medication, write the date discontinued on the log.
8. If a child does not receive his medicine, then this is considered a medication incident. On the log, <u>circle</u> the time the medication was to be given and <u>write</u> in the comment section: medication not given and include your signature. *Complete a medication incident report.*

Refer to the Sample "Medication Log" form

Remember: IF IT IS NOT WRITTEN, IT DID NOT HAPPEN!

DO NOT INDUCE VOMITING
UNLESS INSTRUCTED BY POISON CONTROL.
POISON CONTROL NUMBER 1-800-222-1222

Medication Incidents

A medication incident is a mistake made by a health care provider, caregiver or parent during the process of prescribing, transcribing, dispensing, administering, or using a medication. Most medication incidents occur prior to the actual administration of medication.

Omission or forgetting to give a dose of medicine is the most common medication incident in schools and child care programs.

Medication Incident: "a Violation of the "Five Rights"

A medication incident is any situation that involves the following:

- Forgetting to give a dose of medication.
- Giving more than one dose of the medication.
- Giving the medication at the wrong time.
- Giving the wrong dose.
- Giving the wrong medication.
- Giving the medication to the wrong child.
- Giving the medication by the wrong route.
- Forgetting to document the medication.

Note: Medication may be given 30 minutes before or 30 minutes after the prescribed time, more than that is considered an incident.

Medication Incident Report

CALL Poison Control (1-800-222-1222) when a medication is given to the wrong child or if an overdose of medication is suspected.

1. Document the medication incident on a *"Medication Incident Report"* form. The person responsible for the incident completes the report. If that is not possible, the person who found the incident completes the written report.
2. Record the incident and observations on the child's medication log. *Remember that the medication incident report is a record for the program and not intended for the child's permanent record.*
3. Report medication incidents immediately to the RN consultant, the parent child's health care provider, and other appropriate program staff.
4. Observe the child, record and report any changes.

Refer to the Sample "Medication Incident Report Form"

Preventing Medication Incidents

When a child requires medicine, school and child care personnel become a part of the "drug therapy chain". We expect and trust that this chain assures the right medication has been prescribed, dispensed and administered by the physicians, pharmacists, nurses and other caregivers.

But when humans are involved, mistakes can happen. Anyone in this chain can make an incident because of not doing the right thing or not knowing the correct thing to do. It is the nurses' and caregivers' responsibility to make sure it is understood what the medication is for, how it looks, and how it should be taken.

**Triple checking information about a medication
must occur every time.**

Medication Review

Refer to the Sample Forms Section for the "Medication Administration Onsite Checklist"

Using some type of review process within the school or child care program can help identify problematic areas. Using the Medication Administration Onsite Checklist can provide a format for that review. Ideally reviews for a program should occur at least 2 times during the year. It is a good way for the school nurse or child care health consultant delegating medications to provide meaningful ongoing supervision of the administration of medication. Family child care providers can do this review on their own.

Field Trips
A medication-trained person should accompany children with medications on field trips. The term 'field trip', describes an activity or event which takes place during normal program hours at a location other than the usual program location. Medication administration during extra-curricular activities or overnight activities are not included in this training, but may be addressed by the nurse trainer using specific guidelines and policies.

Student notes

This is a safety checklist to help reduce the chance of making a mistake.

RIGHT CHILD – Protect Confidentiality

- Double check, is this the right child?
- Check the name on the medication label against the permission form.
- Check the child's identity with another staff person.
- Ask the child his name.
- If possible, verify the child's identity by using the child's picture, stapled to the medication log.

RIGHT MEDICATION

- Medications must be given from a properly labeled original bottle. *Check the label three times.*
- First when it is removed from the secured cabinet.
- Second when the medicine is poured.
- Third when returning the medication to the secured cabinet.

RIGHT DOSE

- Give the **exact amount** of medication specified by the *orders from the person with prescriptive authority and the pharmacy label.*

    Note: 1ml = 1cc

    5ml or 5cc = 1 teaspoon

    3.75 ml or 3.75 cc = ¾ teaspoon

    2.5ml or 2.5 cc = ½ teaspoon

RIGHT TIME

- Check with parent the time when the medication was last given at home.
- Check the medication log for the time the medicine needs to be given.
- Check to see if the medicine has already been given for the current day.
- Plan to give medication up to 30 minutes before or 30 minutes after the scheduled time.

RIGHT ROUTE

- Check the medication order and pharmacy label for the route the medication is to be given, (mouth, inhaled, ear drops, eye drops).

Triple Check These 5 Rights
Each and Every Time You Give Medication.

DOCUMENTATION

- Document everything.
- Maintain a record of all medication administered to children.

Remember: IF IT IS NOT WRITTEN, IT DID NOT HAPPEN!

HOW TO ADMINISTER MEDICATION

<u>Always wash your hands</u> before and after giving medication to a child.

Practice Standard (Universal) Precautions

DO NOT UNDER ANY CIRCUMSTANCES,
GIVE ONE CHILD'S MEDICINE TO ANOTHER CHILD.

How to Administer Oral and Topical Medication
Start with clean hands and clean equipment

Oral Medication

Changing the Medication Form
- Crushing or sprinkling can <u>only</u> be done with written authorization of the health care provider.
- **Never mix medication in prepared baby bottles!**
- If ordered or allowed, mix the dose in a small amount (1-teaspoon) of food or drink, to be sure the child will swallow the entire dose at once.
- NOT ALL medications, however, can be mixed in water or juice. Contact the pharmacist for more information.

Pills / Tablets/ Capsules
- Pour medication into a medicine cup, lid of the bottle, paper towel or a small paper cup.
- Have the child wash his hands, before putting the medication into his mouth. Give 6-8 ounces of water.
- Never refer to medication as **"candy."**

Liquids
- Use a calibrated medicine spoon or cup, syringe, or dropper to measure liquid medications.
- <u>Never</u> use household utensils to measure liquid medication.
- Pour medication from the side opposite the label so the label stays readable.

Medicine Spoon or Cup
- Read cup on a flat surface, at eye level, for accuracy.
- <u>Do not</u> try to measure something for an infant or toddler with a small medicine cup. The amount <u>will not</u> be accurate.
- When using a calibrated spoon or syringe, pour or draw up medication to the appropriate line.
  DO NOT OVER OR UNDER FILL. IT IS IMPORTANT TO BE ACCURATE.

Dropper
- Droppers are included as part of the medicine bottle.
- <u>Only</u> use the dropper that is included with the medicine bottle.
- Withdraw the correct dosage and squeeze the dropper, placing the medicine into the side of the child's mouth.

If the child will be touching the medication, he should also wash his hands.

It is the parent's responsibility to provide the appropriate calibrated measuring device e.g., medicine spoon, dropper or syringe. DO NOT use a kitchen spoon!

Syringe

- Pour a small amount into a paper cup, or any small cup.
- Place the tip of the syringe into the liquid in the cup and pull back on the plunger.
- Avoid air bubbles by keeping the tip below the level of the liquid. Draw up enough to equal dosage amount.
- Pour the remainder of the medicine back into the bottle.
- To give the medicine, slowly squirt small amounts towards the back and side of the child's mouth. Do not squirt towards the back of the throat. This will cause gagging.
- <u>For an infant</u>: drop into a nipple for them to suck. Always follow with a bottle. NEVER mix medications with an entire bottle.

Note: Medication may be prescribed in teaspoons, ccs, and mls. Check carefully for the appropriate line measurement on the cup, dropper or syringe.

1cc = 1ml   5cc or 5ml = 1 teaspoon

Make Sure the Child Takes All of the Medicine!

Refusal or Vomiting of Medication

- If the child does not take all of the medication, spits part of it out, vomits or refuses to take part of the medication, **do not give another dose**.
- Contact the child's parent or guardian and request further instructions from the health care provider.

Topical Medication

- Wear gloves when applying topical medications. After use dispose of them and any contaminated dressings in a plastic lined covered container.
- Keep topical medications separate from oral medications.
- Read instructions carefully to avoid mixing up eye and ear drops.

Eye Drops

- Rub medication bottle between the palms of your hand to help warm drops.
- Clean child's eye by wiping each eye once from the inside to the outside. Use a clean tissue for each eye.
- Place child on her back if younger than five. You may need an
- assistant.
- If older than five the child may be seated.
- Ask child to look up, then gently open eye, pull down the lower lid to make a pocket.
- Bring the medicine toward the eye outside the child's field of vision.
- Do not touch the eye or anything else with the bottle or dropper.
- With bottle no more than an inch above the eye, drop one drop into the lower lid.
- Close the eye. Apply pressure on the inside corner of eye for 10-20 seconds.
- Wipe away any excess medication or tearing with clean tissue.

Helpful hint:
A syringe adapter is a plastic device that fits on the medicine bottle. This is an easy way to draw the amount from the bottle with a syringe.

Hold infants in the cradle position to administer oral medication.
Allow toddlers to sit up in a high chair.

Eye Ointments *(follow instructions for eye drops)*
- Applied along the inside of the lower eyelid.
- Rotate the tube when you reach edge of the outer eye, this will help detach the ointment from the tube.
- After applying hold the eye open for a few seconds, and then have the child keep it closed for about 1 minute.
- Wipe away any excess medication or tearing with clean tissue.

Ear Drops
- Rub medication bottle between the palms of your hand to warm drops.
- Have child lie down with affected ear facing up.
- Child <u>younger than three years old</u>, hold ear lobe and pull down and back.
- Child <u>older than three years old</u>, hold upper part of ear lobe and pull up and back.
- A child older than five may sit in a chair and tilt head with affected ear facing up.
- Clean ear with cotton and discard.
- <u>Note</u>: If you see blood or pus, do not administer the drops and notify the RN consultant and parent.
- Drop medication on the side of ear canal. Do not touch the dropper to the ear.
- Have child stay on his side for several minutes.
- You may place a dampened cotton ball loosely in the ear canal if the instructions say to do so.

NEVER INSERT Q-TIPS OR COTTON BALLS <u>INTO</u> THE EAR CANAL!

Skin Creams/ Ointments
- Always use *Standard (Universal) Precautions*. Dispose of gloves after use in a plastic lined container out of reach of children.
- Apply cream or ointment with an applicator to affected area. Use a small amount to cover the area and rub onto the skin.
- If instructions state to cover, place the medicine on the dressing, then cover the area with the dressing.

New application techniques and devices may be introduced. Carefully follow label instructions when applying any type of topical medication. Contact a pharmacist, your school nurse or nurse consultant if you have any questions about application instructions.

Lightning Source UK Ltd.
Milton Keynes UK
UKHW030755210219
337761UK00006B/233/P